United States Government Accountability Office

Report to the Chairman, Committee on the Budget, House of Representatives

I0448161

September 2013

FEDERAL USER FEES

Fee Design Options and Implications for Managing Revenue Instability

September 2013

FEDERAL USER FEES

Fee Design Options and Implications for Managing Revenue Instability

![GAO Highlights logo]

Highlights of GAO-13-820, a report to the Chairman, Committee on the Budget, House of Representatives.

Why GAO Did This Study

In 2012, the President's Budget reported nearly $300 billion collected in user fees from the public. Given the nation's fiscal condition it is critical that every funding source and spending decision be carefully considered and applied to its best use. GAO was asked to review oversight opportunities for fees. GAO examined (1) key Congressional design decisions and related implications for achieving the desired balance between agency flexibility and congressional control, (2) issues related to identifying and managing unobligated balances in selected fee-funded agencies, and (3) key questions to identify potential sources of fee revenue instability and to manage any consequences. To do so, GAO analyzed laws, agency documents and guidance, literature, and prior GAO work. In addition, GAO interviewed officials at three fully fee-funded agencies, which were selected to illustrate implications of key design options, unobligated fee balances, and approaches for managing revenue instability. GAO also validated certain findings with budget subject matter specialists.

What GAO Recommends

GAO is not making any new recommendations in this report. GAO previously recommended that the Office of Management and Budget (OMB) review fee-funded programs and identify opportunities to improve their design and better align fee collections with program costs. OMB has not yet taken action on this recommendation. Two of the three selected fully fee-funded agencies provided technical comments which were incorporated as appropriate.

View GAO-13-820. For more information, contact Susan J. Irving at (202) 512-6806 or irvings@gao.gov or Jacqueline M. Nowicki at (617) 788-0580 or nowick j@gao.gov.

What GAO Found

GAO identified six key fee design decisions related to how fees are set, used, and reviewed that, in the aggregate, enable Congress to design fees that strike the desired balance between agency flexibility and congressional control (see figure below). For example, narrowly limiting the activities for which fees may be used heightens congressional control over the funds; however, doing so can also reduce an agency's flexibility to reallocate resources as needs change and may increase administrative costs. Design decisions also have program management implications. For example, the frequency of fee reviews and adjustments affects the alignment between collections and costs. Failing to review fees regularly has sometimes resulted in large increases when fees are eventually updated, creating costly challenges. Understanding the implications of fee design is important to avoid such unintended consequences.

Congressional Fee Design Decisions Key to Determining Agency Flexibility and Congressional Control

Setting	Using				Reviewing
How are fee rates set?	What Congressional action triggers the use of fee collections?	What is the period of availability for the collections?	For what purposes may the collections be used?	To what degree will Congress limit the amount of collections that can be used?	What types of reporting and oversight requirements are in place?

Source: GAO.

Identifying and understanding unobligated balances—the portion of obligational authority that has not yet been obligated—in fee-based accounts is challenging. There is no single list of all federal user fees, and in general, budget accounts are not labeled in a way that indicates whether an account contains fee collections. This makes it challenging to identify whether (or which) unobligated balances in an account are fee-related. Further, some fee designs include dedicated reserves that appear as unobligated balances. Despite these challenges, funding a program or agency through fees does not eliminate the need for careful monitoring and managing of unobligated balances.

Considering key questions about costs and collections can enable Congress and agencies to identify and manage potential fluctuations in fee collections–known as revenue instability–as well as potential consequences. Importantly, decision makers need to understand potential vulnerabilities in the context of a fee's design. Examples of such questions include: what is the risk that fee revenue instability will affect a program? What analysis is needed to understand factors such as cost drivers and elements that influence collections? Are there data limitations that could add uncertainty to collection estimates? Can the agency quickly respond to changing costs? What factors affect the timing and pattern of collections and spending? If revenue instability is a function of a fee's design, the most sustainable solutions are often found by realigning costs and collections. In other cases, maintaining a reserve can help address sudden or temporary fluctuations in collections and/or costs and can minimize the effect of revenue instability on operations.

Contents

Figures

Abbreviations

AIA	Leahy-Smith America Invents Act of 2011
APHIS	Animal and Plant Health Inspection Service
AQI	Agricultural Quarantine Inspection
CBP	Customs and Border Protection
CBO	Congressional Budget Office
CFO Act	Chief Financial Officers Act of 1990
COBRA	Consolidated Omnibus Reconciliation Act of 1985
FCC	Federal Communications Commission
IOAA	Independent Offices Appropriation Act of 1952
OMB	Office of Management and Budget
PEF	Public Enterprise Fund
Mint	United States Mint
USAC	Universal Service Administrative Company
USCIS	United States Citizenship and Immigration Service
USF	Universal Service Fund
USPTO	United States Patent and Trademark Office

GAO

U.S. GOVERNMENT ACCOUNTABILITY OFFICE

441 G St. N.W.
Washington, DC 20548

September 30, 2013

The Honorable Paul Ryan
Chairman
Committee on the Budget
House of Representatives

Dear Mr. Chairman:

In 2012, the federal government collected nearly $300 billion in user fees from the public.[1] Given the nation's fiscal condition, it is critical that every funding source and spending decision be carefully considered and applied to its best use.[2] As funds become increasingly scarce and new policy priorities emerge, policymakers have demonstrated interest in user fees as a means of financing new and existing services. Well designed fees can fund programs or activities that benefit an identifiable population beyond what is normally provided to the public, while promoting economic efficiency and equity.

You asked us to provide information on the key appropriations frameworks used to design federal user fees and charges, on the unobligated balances in selected fee accounts—specifically, the portion of obligational authority that has not yet been obligated—and on some key questions Congress and agencies could consider when overseeing and managing fee revenue instability. Our objectives were (1) to identify the key Congressional design decisions and related implications for achieving the desired balance between agency flexibility and Congressional control, (2) to examine issues related to identifying and managing unobligated balances in selected fee-funded agencies, and (3) to identify key questions to identify potential sources of fee revenue instability and manage any consequences.

---

[1] User charges from the public as reported in *The President's Fiscal Year 2014 Budget Analytical Perspectives.*

[2] We have also identified the key considerations for evaluating carryover balances in non-fee accounts. See GAO, *Budget Issues: Key Questions to Consider When Evaluating Balances in Federal Accounts,* GAO-13-798 (Washington, D.C.: Sept. 30, 2013).

To identify the key Congressional design decisions for achieving the desired levels of agency flexibility and Congressional control, we reviewed our prior work, including *Federal User Fees: A Design Guide*,[3] and selected user fee statutory authorities and regulations and met with the Congressional Budget Office. We also reviewed relevant user fee policies contained in the Office of Management and Budget's (OMB) Circular A-25 and contained in the Chief Financial Officers Act of 1990 (CFO Act).[4]

To review unobligated balances derived from fees, we reviewed fiscal year 2007 through 2011 unobligated balance data from OMB's MAX database, agency congressional justifications, and agency financial documents. We also reviewed data from our 2011 survey of fee collections in agencies covered by the CFO Act and OMB Circular A-25 that we collected for our annual review of program duplication, overlap, and fragmentation.[5] In addition, we reviewed congressional budget justifications and financial reports from agencies not covered by the CFO Act. We reviewed the amount of fees collected and the statutory authorities governing collection and use of fees. Based on this, we selected three fully fee-funded agencies— the United States Mint (the Mint) in the Department of the Treasury, the United States Patent and Trademark Office (USPTO) in the Department of Commerce, and the Federal Communications Commission (FCC). Although the results from these three agencies may not be generalized to all fee-funded agencies, the selection of these agencies was appropriate to illustrate implications of key design options, of fee unobligated balances, and of approaches for managing revenue instability. For each of these three agencies, we reviewed agency annual reports and financial statements; we also reviewed agency fee collection procedures, policies, and data. We spoke with agency officials about their management of fee collections. To assess the reliability of OMB's MAX data, and data on unobligated balances that we received from FCC, we reviewed available

---

[3]GAO, *Federal User Fees: A Design Guide*, GAO-08-386SP (Washington, D.C.: May 29, 2008).

[4] Chief Financial Officers Act of 1990, Pub. L. No. 101-576 (Nov. 15, 1990), *codified at*, 31 U.S.C. § 902.

[5] GAO, *2012 Annual Report: Opportunities to Reduce Duplication, Overlap and Fragmentation, Achieve Savings, and Enhance Revenue*, GAO-12-342SP (Washington, D.C.: Feb. 28, 2012), 279-284.

documentation and followed up as needed to resolve any questions. Based on our review, we found these data sufficiently reliable for the purposes of our report.

To develop the key questions for managing revenue instability, we reviewed our past work on federal user fees—including our user fee design guide and reviews of specific fees—and considered our current audit work in the three selected agencies noted above. We also reviewed literature from governmental and nongovernmental organizations to identify common principles for managing reserve funds. Specifically, we used published guidance from a state government, from professional associations, and from a consulting firm that described practices in managing reserve funds; these sources were selected from a literature review, based upon their applicability to a federal fee-funded framework. Once we identified common themes in fee-funded programs that were experiencing revenue instability, and identified leading practices for creating and managing reserve funds, we developed a set of questions that agency managers and Congress could use to identify and manage fee revenue instability. We validated our key questions with subject matter specialists selected for their fee program expertise in both the public and private sectors, as well as with relevant officials at USPTO, the Mint, the FCC, and OMB.

We performed our work from August 2012 to September 2013 in accordance with generally accepted government auditing standards. Those standards require that we plan and perform the audit to obtain sufficient, appropriate evidence to provide a reasonable basis for our findings and conclusions based on our audit objectives. We believe that the evidence obtained provides a reasonable basis for our findings and conclusions based on our audit objectives.

Background

In general, a user fee is related to some voluntary transaction or request for government goods or services, above and beyond what is normally available to the public (such as a national park entrance fee or a license to operate a radio station). We have previously reported on the characteristics (equity, efficiency, revenue adequacy, and administrative burden) that can influence the effectiveness of user fees to fund activities that provide benefits to identifiable users.[6]

User fee designs can vary widely and, in general, are governed by two authorities: an authority to charge fees, and an authority to use fee collections. Agencies derive their authority to charge fees either from the Independent Offices Appropriation Act of 1952 (IOAA) or from a specific statutory authority.[7] Overall, fees established under the IOAA must be (1) fair and (2) based on costs to the government, on the value of the service or thing to the recipient, on public policy, or on interest serviced. Agencies that established fees under the IOAA, however, are only authorized to charge the fee; a separate authority is required to use the fee collections. However, Congress has frequently provided agencies with the authority via authorizing or appropriations legislation both to collect fees and to use the collections. In these specific fee authorities, Congress determines the degree of flexibility to make fee design and implementation decisions that will be retained or delegated to the agency.

Regardless how the imposition of fee collections is authorized, Congressional action is required for agencies to use those collections. Congress may provide agencies with the authority to collect and use a fee within authorizing legislation, within appropriations legislation, or within both.[8] For agencies whose fee collections are available for obligation on a no-year or multi-year authority basis, unobligated balances can be carried forward from year to year. To illustrate the reasons why such balances exist in fee-related programs, we selected three fee-funded agencies with unobligated balances: the United States Mint (Mint), the United States Patent and Trademark Office (USPTO), and the Federal Communications Commission (FCC).

---

[6]GAO-08-386SP.

[7]Without additional statutory authority to retain collections, fees collected under the IOAA are deposited in the general fund of the U.S. Treasury and are generally not available to the agency or the activity generating the fees. IOAA requires that agency regulations establishing a user fee are subject to policies prescribed by the President. OMB provides such guidance to executive branch agencies under this authority through OMB Circular No. A-25.

[8]Depending on the type of legislation providing the authority to collect or spend the fees, these funds are either mandatory or discretionary. Collections authorized in authorizing legislation are considered mandatory and collections that are authorized in appropriations legislation are discretionary.

Table 1: Three Agencies Selected to Illustrate Reasons for Unobligated Balances in Fee Accounts

The United States Patent and Trademark Office (USPTO)	USPTO is a component of the Department of Commerce and is charged with examining applications and granting patents to new, useful, and non-obvious inventions and with reviewing and registering marks—trademarks, service marks, certification marks, and collective membership marks. USPTO is fully funded by fee collections paid by applicants and owners applying for and maintaining patents or trademarks. The fees correspond to products and services at different points in patent and trademark application and examination processes and lifecycles. The Leahy-Smith America Invents Act (AIA)[a] of 2011 provides USPTO the authority to set all fee amounts through the regulatory process. USPTO is authorized to spend the fee amounts collected each year, up to the amount appropriated by Congress. The AIA also created a special account called the Patent and Trademark Fee Reserve Fund, referred to as the FRF by USPTO. Any USPTO collections in excess of the amounts annually appropriated by Congress are deposited into this fund. The USPTO can access money from the Patent and Trademark Fee Reserve Fund only to the extent appropriated by Congress. We reported in 2012 that 90 percent of USPTO's revenues came from patent fees, and the remainder of revenue came from trademark fees.
The United States Mint (Mint)	The Mint, a component of the Department of the Treasury, manufactures and distributes coins and medals. It provides circulating coins to the Federal Reserve for distribution to banks, and prepares and distributes numismatic items, including investment-grade bullion coins and high-quality versions of circulating coinage, precious metal coins, commemorative coins, medals, and sets. It is also responsible for safeguarding noncirculating coins and medals and the precious metals used to make them. In 1995, Congress created the United States Mint Public Enterprise Fund (PEF), which accounts for all receipts and expenses related to production and sale of numismatic items and circulating coinage, as well as protection activities. Since establishment of the PEF, the Mint has operated without direct appropriations, and is entirely funded by its collections. Any amounts in the PEF that are determined by the Mint to be in excess of the amount required for Mint expenses are transferred to the Treasury's General Fund. From fiscal years 2006 to 2010 the Mint returned collections between $388 million and $825 million annually to the General Fund. In fiscal year 2012 the Mint collected $3.4 billion in revenue from the sale of circulating and noncirculating items. Numismatic coins, including gold and silver bullion coins, generated approximately 86 percent of the Mint's revenues; sales of circulating coins generated 14 percent.

The Federal Communications Commission (FCC)	The FCC is an independent regulatory agency governed by five commissioners appointed by the President and confirmed by the Senate. It is charged with regulating interstate and international communications by radio, television, wire, satellite, and cable, and with regulating telecommunications services for all people of the United States. The FCC is authorized by Section 9 of the Communications Act of 1934 (as amended) to assess and collect regulatory fees to recover the regulatory costs associated with the Commission's enforcement, policy- and rulemaking, user information, and international activities;[b] it is subject to annual Congressional appropriations that specify the amount of regulatory fees it may collect each year. In addition, the FCC manages the Universal Service Fund (USF), which was created by the Telecommunications Act of 1996.[c] This fund is administered by the Universal Service Administrative Company (USAC), an independent, not-for-profit corporation designated as the administrator of the federal USF by the FCC, and financed by mandatory contributions from U.S. telecommunications service providers and other providers of telecommunications. The USAC provides USF funds directly to service providers to defray the cost of serving customers in high cost and rural areas, and of serving customers who have low incomes. In addition, USF funds provide financial support to assist schools, libraries, and health care providers in purchasing telecommunications services, advanced telecommunications and information services, and Internet access. In fiscal 2012, the FCC collected $340 million in the form of regulatory fees which were deposited into the FCC's salaries and expense account, and $9.3 billion in the form of contributions for the USF, which were deposited in the USF account administered by USAC.[d]

Source: USPTO, the Mint, and FCC.
Notes: (a) Leahy-Smith America Invents Act of 2011, P.L. 112-29. § 10 (Sept. 16, 2011).

(b) Pub. L. No. 73-416, section 9 is codified at 47 U.S.C. § 159. FCC also collects application fees from companies for activities such as license applications, renewals or requests for modification. These fees are deposited in the General Fund of the Treasury and cannot be used by the FCC. 47 U.S.C. § 158(e).
(c) Pub. L. No. 104-104, codified at 47 U.S.C. § 254.
(d) The remaining revenue collected was from contributions to the Telecommunications Relay Service Fund, and proceeds from radio spectrum auctions and the North American Numbering Plan.

Fee Design Affects the Balance between Congressional Control and Agency Flexibility and Has Implications for Program Management

Congress Delegates or Retains Varying Degrees of Decision-Making Authority Depending on How It Designs Key Aspects of User Fees

When designing fees, Congress is presented with a number of decisions regarding how a fee will be set, collected, used, and reviewed. At each decision point, Congress can delegate some flexibility to agencies, or it can retain that control. In the aggregate, these decisions enable Congress to design a fee that strikes its desired balance between agency flexibility and Congressional control. It is important to note that regardless of how Congress designs a fee, it always retains oversight over the fee and over the goods and services the fee supports. Figure 1 identifies six key fee design decisions for Congress that have a direct bearing on how much control Congress will retain and how much flexibility will be delegated to an agency.[9] For each design question, we have identified at least two options, one granting the agency more flexibility and the other retaining more control for Congress. In some cases, Congress selects an option that falls in between the two options shown in figure 1. For example, Congress can grant an agency the authority to set some of its fee rates by regulation while setting other fees, or requirements for any of the rates such as provisions for exemptions, waivers, and caps, in statute.

---

[9]There are other Congressional design decisions that are not included in figure 1. These decisions have less direct bearing on the amount of agency flexibility or the nature of congressional control. For example, Congress could specify how an agency should collect its fees in some cases, but might delegate that decision to the agency in other cases. However, the Department of the Treasury established government-wide guidance directing agencies to use electronic collections in the absence of specific Congressional direction. As a result of this executive direction, even when Congress delegates the collection method to the agency, the implication for increased agency flexibility is generally less significant.

GAO-13-820 Federal User Fees

Figure 1: Key Fee Design Decisions Allow for Agency Flexibility or Congressional Control

Directions:

Mouse over entries in the table below for additional information

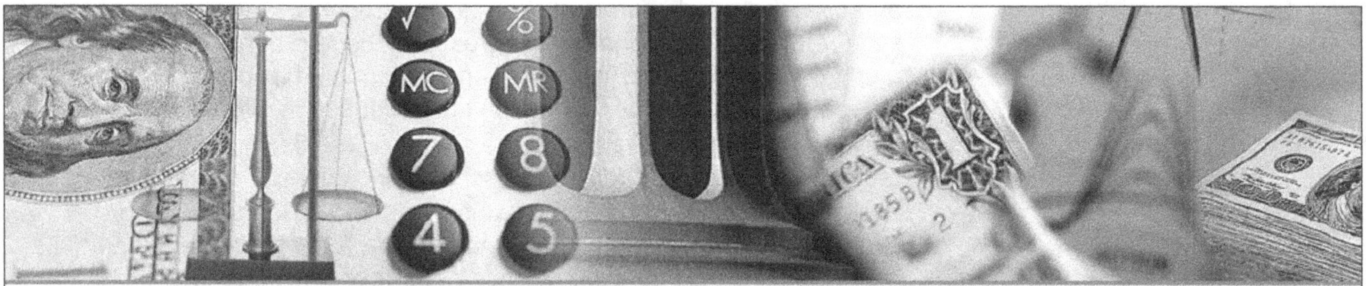

	Key design questions	Options increasing agency flexibility	Options increasing congressional control
Setting	How are fee rates set?	By regulation	In statute
Using	What Congressional action triggers the use of fee collections?	Offsetting collection authority	Offsetting receipt authority Government receipt authority
	What is the period of availability for the collections?	No year	Limited year
	For what purposes may the collections be used?	Broadly defined uses	Narrowly defined uses
	To what degree will Congress limit the amount of collections that can be used?	No limit	Limit set in statute
Reviewing	What types of reporting and oversight requirements are in place?	Basic requirements such as CFO Act Biennial Fee Reviews	Additional requirements

Source: GAO.

[a]GAO-08-386SP.

Print instructions | To print full text version of this graphic, go to appendix I.

Fee Design Options Have Implications for Fee Program Management

Congress's fee design decisions have implications for fee program management beyond striking the desired balance between agency flexibility and Congressional control. Below, we discuss in more detail the key fee design options introduced in figure 1—setting, using, and reviewing—and the implications that flow from decisions about each design option. Understanding these implications, especially in the context of Congress's own priorities and goals, can help to avoid unintended consequences in fee design.

Implications of Fee Design: Setting

Figure 2 shows the key design options related to how fee rates are set.

Figure 2: Key Fee Design Options: Setting

	Key design questions	Options increasing agency flexibility	Options increasing congressional control
Setting	How are fee rates set?	By regulation	In statute

Source: GAO.

Note: See interactive figure on page 8 for more details.

The frequency of fee review and adjustment, and the ability to keep fees and costs aligned, have a number of potential implications for agencies. The CFO Act[10] requires federal agencies to review user fees biennially

---

[10] The CFO Act requires agencies to review "fees, royalties, rents, and other charges imposed by the agency for services and things of value it provides." For the purposes of this discussion, GAO refers to all of these collectively as user fees.

and OMB's Circular A-25 directs agencies to set fees to recover all direct and indirect costs to the federal government of a good or service. We have previously reported that the failure to review fees regularly can result in large fee increases when the fees are eventually updated, which creates costly challenges.[11] For example, the U.S. Citizenship and Immigration Service (USCIS) is authorized to charge fees for the adjudication of immigration and naturalization applications. Although USCIS has the authority to adjust its fees through the regulatory process, in 2007 it conducted its first comprehensive fee review in nine years.[12] As a result, USCIS had to increase fees by an average of 86 percent to align them with its costs.[13]   During the month before the fee increase took effect, the number of applications received increased an unprecedented 100 percent over the prior month, far outpacing the agency's processing capacity. This contributed to a backlog of 1.47 million applications and unplanned costs to secure additional facilities to store these applications. In 2012, we found that prior to the passage of the AIA, fees generating over 80 percent of the USPTO's revenues were set in statute.[14] This limited the USPTO's ability to adjust fee rates as costs changed. Other than periodic increases to reflect inflation, these statutorily-set fees had not been reviewed or adjusted for the 7 years before 2012.

In contrast, there are other examples of intentional deviation from cost-fee alignment. In some cases, a less precise alignment between costs and each fee is chosen in order to achieve a policy or administrative goal. A fully fee-funded agency covers program costs in the aggregate, but not

---

[11]GAO, *Federal User Fees: Additional Analyses and Timely Reviews Could Improve Immigration and Naturalization User Fee Design and USCIS Operations*, GAO-09-180 (Washington, D.C.: Jan. 23, 2009).

[12] USCIS issued a subsequent fee review in 2010.

[13] In 2009 we found that USCIS's fees did not include the costs of certain retirement benefits paid by the Office of Personnel Management and the costs of the Department of Treasury's lockbox services—where some applications were received and processed. In response to our recommendation, USCIS identified these costs in its 2010 fee review. However, USCIS did not include these costs in setting its fees and the Office of Management and Budget concurred with USCIS's decision. See GAO, *Immigration Applications Fees: Costing Methodology Improvements Would Provide More Reliable Basis for Setting Fees*, GAO-09-70. (Washington, D.C.: Jan. 23, 2009).

[14] GAO, *Patent and Trademark Office: New User Fee Design Presents Opportunities to Build on Transparency and Communication Success*, GAO-12-514R (Washington, D.C.: Apr. 25, 2012).

necessarily on a fee-by-fee basis. For example, within the suite of USCIS's immigration and naturalization fees, Congress directed that fees providing adjudication and naturalization services be set to ensure recovery of full costs of providing such services. This includes the costs of similar services provided without charge to asylum applicants or other immigrants.[15] As a result, the costs of processing applicants granted the fee waivers are distributed to other fee payers as a flat-rate surcharge. However, unintentional misalignment between fees and costs can increase the demand for more expensive services, because fee payers do not bear the agency's total cost of the service. This can result in some fee payers subsidizing others with no public policy purpose.

We have found over the years that fees set through the regulatory process may be updated more frequently than fees set in statute: therefore, they may more consistently align collections with costs.[16] However, we have also previously reported that, in the past, stakeholders expressed concern about the agency incentive to inflate costs or the lack of incentive to restrain costs.[17] This risk may be reduced, and tools for Congressional and stakeholder oversight may be enhanced, if the agency clearly reports its methods for setting the fee, including an accounting of program costs and the assumptions it uses to project future program costs and fee collections. Further, federal agencies must also follow guidelines regarding their cost accounting information, providing some safeguards against artificial inflation of program costs.[18]

Implications of Fee Design: Using

Figure 3 shows the key design options related to an agency's access to and use of its fee collections.

---

[15]The use of fee waivers is one method of incorporating the ability-to-pay principle of equity in a fee design. See GAO-08-386SP and GAO-09-180.

[16]For examples, see GAO-08-386SP and GAO-12-514R.

[17]GAO-08-386SP.

[18]Federal Accounting Standards Advisory Board, *Statement of Federal Financial Accounting Standards No. 4: Managerial Cost Accounting Standards and Concepts* (July 31, 1995). Cost information can be used by Congress and federal executives in making decisions about allocating federal resources, authorizing and modifying programs, and evaluating program performance; it can also be used by program managers in making managerial decisions to improve operating economy and efficiency.

Figure 3: Key Fee Design Options: Using

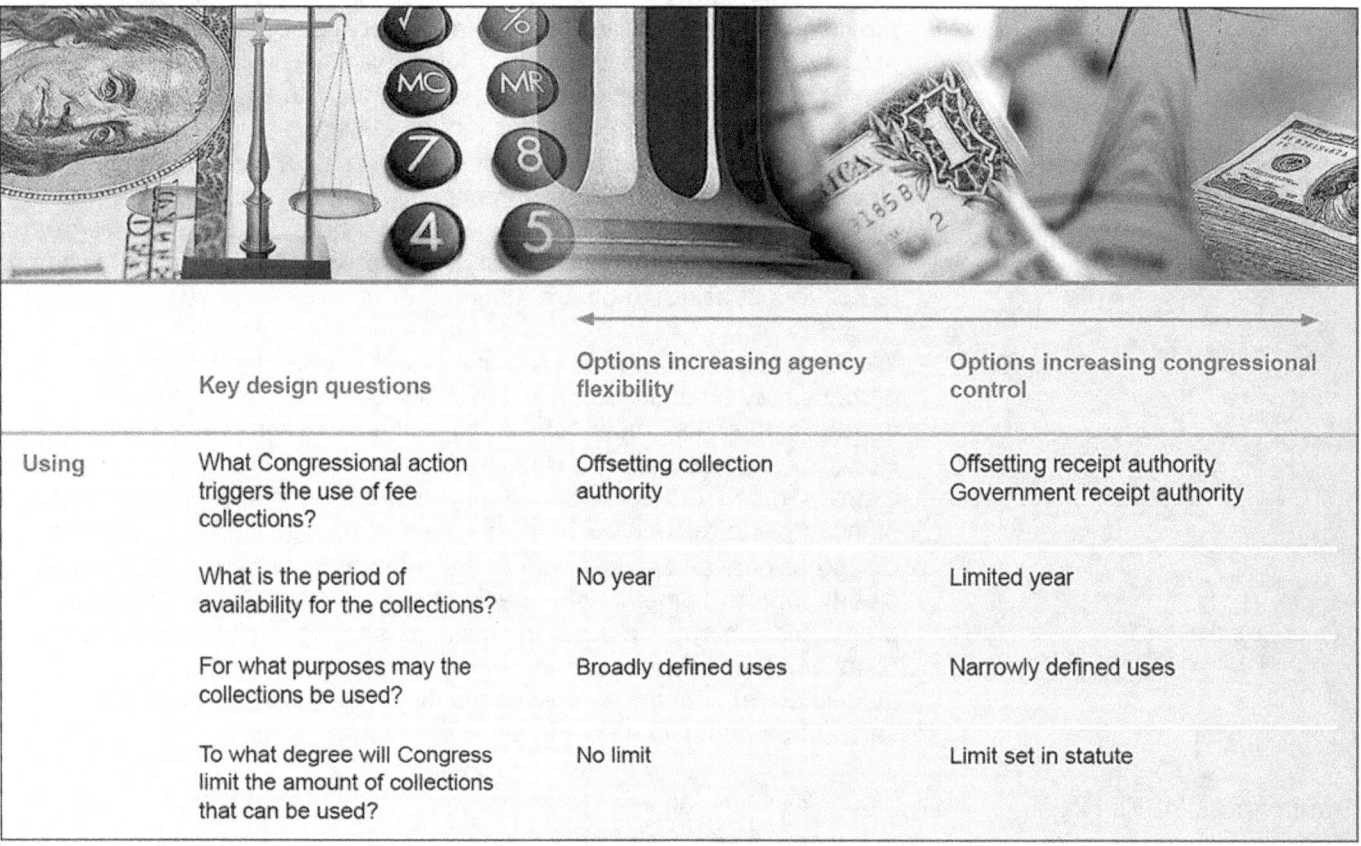

	Key design questions	Options increasing agency flexibility	Options increasing congressional control
Using	What Congressional action triggers the use of fee collections?	Offsetting collection authority	Offsetting receipt authority Government receipt authority
	What is the period of availability for the collections?	No year	Limited year
	For what purposes may the collections be used?	Broadly defined uses	Narrowly defined uses
	To what degree will Congress limit the amount of collections that can be used?	No limit	Limit set in statute

Source: GAO.

Note: See interactive figure on page 8 for more details.

Congressional decisions about the collection and use of a fee will determine how the fee will be considered within the context of all federal budgetary resources. Fee collections are classified into 3 categories: offsetting collections, offsetting receipts, or governmental receipts.[19] As noted in figure 1, fees classified as offsetting collections can provide agencies with more flexibility because they are generally available for

---

[19]The Budget Enforcement Act of 1990, defines offsetting collections and receipts as negative budget authority and the reductions to it as positive authority.

agency obligation without an additional annual appropriation. In contrast, offsetting receipts and governmental receipts offer greater Congressional control because, generally, additional Congressional action is needed before the collections are available for agency obligation. Regular Congressional review—whether through reauthorization or the annual appropriations process—offers opportunities to exercise Congressional oversight. Regardless of the specific classification, all fees remain subject to Congressional oversight at any point in time.

The authorities under which an agency may collect and use fees can be affected by different legislative decisions made over time, resulting in increased complexity and potentially significant intended or unintended effects. For example, a program's authorizing legislation may grant the agency the authority to collect fees but not provide the agency the authority to spend the fees. As a result, any later enacted legislation to allow the agency to spend the fees may not be consistent with the authorizing legislation, contributing to increased complexity.

Congress also determines the period of time the collections are available for obligation, the purposes for which they may be used, and the amount of collections that are available to the agency—thereby determining how much flexibility the agency has in managing its fee collections.

Time. When Congress limits the period of availability of funds, it retains greater control over when the funds will be used. When Congress provides an agency unlimited access to its fee collections (that is, makes the fee collections available until they are expended) agencies have greater flexibility and can carry over unobligated amounts to future fiscal years. This enables agencies to align fees and costs over a longer horizon and to better prepare for, and adjust to, fluctuations in collections and costs. Carrying over unobligated balances from year to year, if an agency has multi- or no-year fee collections, is one way a reserve can be established. Set aside or reserved funds can sustain operations in the event of a sharp downturn in collections or increase in costs. We have previously found that, for programs where fees are expected to cover all or most program costs, and especially when program costs do not necessarily decline with a drop in fee collections, a reserve is important.[20]

---

[20]GAO, *Federal User Fees: Substantive Reviews Needed to Align Port-Related Fees with the Programs They Support*, GAO-08-321 (Washington, D.C.: Feb. 22, 2008).

(Later in this report, we will discuss reserve funds at fee-funded agencies.)

Purpose. Congress can also specify limits on the activities or purposes for which an agency may use fee collections. Congress has granted some agencies broad authority to use some of the fees they collect for any program purpose, but has limited the use of other fees to specific sets of activities. Such restrictions may benefit stakeholders and increase Congressional control. For example, according to USPTO officials, patent fee collections can only be used for patent processes, and trademark fee collections can only be used for trademark processes, as well as the proportionate share of the administrative costs of the agency. USPTO officials stated that patent and trademark customers are typically two distinct groups and this division helps to assure stakeholders that their fees are supporting the activities that affect them directly.

On the other hand, statutes that too narrowly limit how fees can be used reduces both Congress's flexibility to make resource decisions and an agency's flexibility to reallocate resources. This can make it more difficult to pursue public policy goals or respond to changing program needs, such as when the activities intended to achieve fee-funded purposes change. For example, Customs and Border Protection's (CBP) Merchandise Processing Fee is authorized to fund only a specific set of activities. However, after the events of September 11, 2001, as the program's focus shifted towards security, other activities (such as screening and inspecting conveyances and inspecting vessels and containers) became part of the program. While CBP views these activities as part of the merchandise processing service, they are not included in the set of authorized activities that may be funded by the fee collections; the result is a misalignment between the services provided and the authorized uses for the fees.

Narrowing the authorized uses of a fee in statute can also increase agency administrative costs. For example, the narrower the subset of activities for which collections can be used, the more detailed and potentially expensive the required cost accounting. Given these challenges, more frequent reviews and updated fee schedules become even more important to ensure that the authorized purposes remain aligned with program needs. For example, in 2008 we reported that some CBP inspection fees can pay for only some inspection activities and only under certain circumstances. In order to be reimbursed for time spent on authorized activities for various fees, CBP must track the time spent on these activities for several of its inspection fees—including customs, immigration, and agriculture activities.[21] In early 2007, to help address a concern that timekeeping was taking time away from officers' inspection duties, CBP implemented a standard process for tracking the time dedicated for these activities. However, at one port we visited for the 2008 report, on each shift, a full-time CBP officer was assigned solely to tracking staff time. In 2013, we found that CBP still does not capture all of the time spent on agriculture activities in its Cost Management Information System—the system in which CBP tracks its activities and determines personnel costs.[22]

Amount. Congress determines the specific level of budget authority provided for a program's activities by limiting the amount of fee collections that can be collected or used by the agency; however, these limits can also pose challenges for the agency. For example, when the agency is not authorized to retain or use all of its fee collections and no other funding source is provided, the agency may not have the funds available to produce the goods or services that it has promised, or that it is required by law to provide. In a 2012 report, we found that in USPTO's case, fees must be designed to recover costs of the related activities in aggregate as directed by the AIA.[23] However, with each set of application fees collected, USPTO takes on an additional work activity. In some years Congress chose not to make available to USPTO the full amount of its collections to support that work.[24] USPTO officials stated that, prior to the passage of the AIA, this contributed to USPTO's inability to hire sufficient examiners to keep up with USPTO's workload and invest in needed

---

[21]GAO-08-321.

[22]GAO, *Agricultural Quarantine Inspection Fees: Major Changes Needed to Align Fee Revenues with Program Costs*, GAO-13-268 (Washington, D.C.: March 1, 2013).

[23]GAO-12-514R.

[24]Prior to enactment of the AIA, all fees collected were deposited into USPTO's account and were available to the extent appropriated. Since the enactment of AIA, collections during a fiscal year in excess of the amount appropriated to USPTO for the fiscal year are deposited into the new Patent and Trademark Fee Reserve Fund. As before, these excess collections are available to USPTO only to the extent appropriated by Congress. In 2012 we reported that the establishment of this special account increased transparency of these funds because any amounts appropriated, transferred, or rescinded from the fund would be clearly visible.

technology systems to modernize the USPTO. In 2012, we reported a backlog of over 640,000 patent applications.[25]

Limiting the availability of fee collections may also have future budgetary implications for Congress. For example, as mentioned above, USPTO collections in excess of appropriations are deposited into the Patent and Trademark Fee Reserve Fund and are not available to the agency without additional Congressional action. If these amounts are made available in future years rather than in the year the fees were collected, the action will count or "score" as new budget authority against discretionary spending limits in place in a given future fiscal year, and will not offset against budget authority made available that year. The effect of this scoring may make the fee-funded activities appear more costly and can make granting access to previously collected amounts a less desirable option for Congressional fee designers. The outcome can lead to the buildup of unavailable and unobligated balances.

Implications of Fee Design: Reviewing

Figure 4 shows the design decisions related to the kinds of specific reporting or review requirements Congress may wish to impose, beyond the standard biennial review requirement in the CFO Act.

---

[25]As of July 2013, this backlog has been reduced to approximately 591,000 patent applications.

Figure 4: Key Fee Design Options: Reviewing

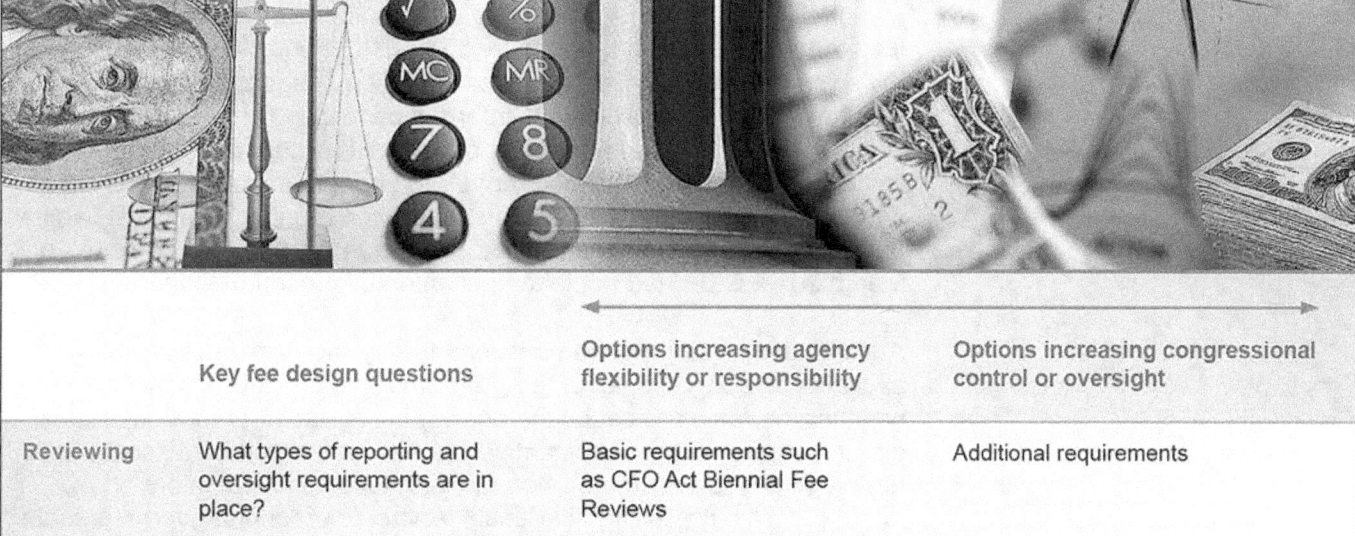

	Key fee design questions	Options increasing agency flexibility or responsibility	Options increasing congressional control or oversight
Reviewing	What types of reporting and oversight requirements are in place?	Basic requirements such as CFO Act Biennial Fee Reviews	Additional requirements

Source: GAO.

Note: See interactive figure on page 8 for more details.

When designing a fee, Congress must balance granting more autonomy to an agency (by requiring no additional reporting and review beyond that required in the CFO Act) with stronger control for itself (via additional reporting and oversight requirements over and above the CFO Act requirements). When a fee's authorizing statute does not specify review and reporting requirements or if a fee derives its statutory authority from the Independent Offices Appropriation Act of 1952,[26] the CFO Act requires and OMB Circular No. A-25 directs agencies to review their fees biennially and to recommend fee adjustments as appropriate. In addition, OMB Circular No. A-25 directs agencies to include non-fee-funded programs in these reviews to determine whether fees should be initiated for government services or goods for which fees are not currently charged. Further, if imposing such fees is prohibited or restricted by law, agencies are to recommend legislative changes as appropriate. Moreover, OMB Circular No. A-25 directs agencies to discuss the results of these reviews and any resulting proposals, such as adjustments to fee

---

[26]Pub. L. No. 82-137 (Aug. 31, 1951), *codified at*, 31 U.S.C. § 9701.

GAO-13-820 Federal User Fees

rates, in annual reports, such as performance and accountability reports. However, our 2011 survey of the 24 agencies covered by the CFO Act and OMB Circular No. A-25 suggested that agencies are reviewing more fees than they are discussing in their annual reports.[27] While these reviews may provide information for agency management and decision making, the extent to which this information is being shared with Congressional decision makers or other stakeholders appears far more limited. In 2012, we concluded that OMB should do more to ensure that agencies comply with requirements and recommended that OMB use its budget reviews to ensure agencies are adhering to this guidance. As of March 2013, OMB had not taken action on this recommendation.[28]

Additional reporting requirements can further increase information available to Congress about fee programs. We previously concluded that whether fee rates are set by the agency in regulation or by Congress in statute, agencies must substantively review and report on all cost-based fees regularly to ensure decision makers have complete information about program costs and activities.[29] A variety of reporting requirements can be included in appropriations, authorizing legislation, or committee reports. For example, AIA requires USPTO to report on the implementation of the AIA, which includes fee-setting authority. In

---

[27]Specifically, 21 of the 23 agencies that responded to our survey reported varying levels of adherence to the biennial review and reporting requirements. The survey responses indicated that for most fees, agencies (1) had not discussed fee review results in annual reports, and (2) had not reviewed the fees and were inconsistent in their ability to provide fee review documentation. The 24th CFO Act agency, the Department of Defense, did not respond to our survey in time to be included. See GAO, *2012 Annual Report: Opportunities to Reduce Duplication, Overlap and Fragmentation, Achieve Savings, and Enhance Revenue,* GAO-12-342SP (Washington, D.C.: Feb. 28, 2012).

[28]GAO, "General Government: Federal User Fees," *GAO's Action Tracker* (Washington, DC: March 6, 2013), accessed July 25, 2013, http://www.gao.gov/duplication/action_tracker/Federal_User_Fees/action1.

[29]GAO-09-180. For example, in 2007 we found that under CBP's authorizing statute for passenger inspection user fees, not all activities that may be funded from the customs fee were necessarily associated with conducting air passenger inspections, and not all inspection activities were reimbursable by funds from the user fee account. We concluded in that report that unless agencies present a comprehensive picture of the fees, including the full scope of inspection activities and their costs, Congress will lack a complete picture of whether the fees work in concert or conflict with each other, which could hamper oversight. See GAO, *Federal User Fees: Key Aspects of International Air Passenger Inspection Fees Should be Addressed Regardless of Whether Fees are Consolidated,* GAO-07-1131 (Washington, D.C.: Sept. 24, 2007).

addition, USPTO's 2012 appropriations required a spending plan to access funds in the Patent and Trademark Fee Reserve Fund. Similarly, the Mint is required to report to Congress biennially on the status of coin production costs, and annually on the operation of the Mint's Numismatic Public Enterprise Fund, as well as provide quarterly financial reports on the Funds.

Reporting requirements sometimes contain requirements to include stakeholders during the course of reviews. For example, in accordance with the AIA, USPTO is required to work with the relevant public advisory committee to hold public hearings on fee-setting, to consider and analyze any comments, advice or recommendations from the advisory committee, and to publish proposed and final rules in the *Federal Register*, including the purpose, rationale, and possible benefits resulting from the change. Our previous work has found that including stakeholders in the fee review process can increase success for substantive, two-way communication and understanding/buy-in on the fee setting process,[30] and that effectively communicating with stakeholders involves sharing relevant analysis and information as well as providing opportunities for stakeholder input.[31]

Agencies Manage Unobligated Balances Differently Depending on Whether They Represent Operating Reserves or Reflect the Timing of Collections and Outlays

Identifying and understanding unobligated balances in fee-based accounts is challenging. There is no single list of all federal user fees. In addition, although some fees are deposited into an account containing only fee collections, others are deposited into accounts that also contain other types of funds such as general fund appropriations. In general, budget accounts are not labeled in a way that indicates whether the account contains fee collections. This also makes it challenging to identify which unobligated balances in an account are related to fee collections. Further, as discussed below, some fee designs include dedicated reserves that appear as unobligated balances. Despite these challenges, unobligated balances must be carefully monitored in agencies funded by fee collections.

---

[30]GAO-08-321 and GAO-07-1131.

[31]GAO-08-386SP.

Table 2: Unobligated Balances of Selected Fee-Funded Agencies, Fiscal Year 2012

	USPTO	Mint	FCC
Unobligated balance	$238 million	$694 million	$3.2 billion
Total budget authority	$2.4 billion	$3.4 billion	$10.5 billion
Unobligated balances as a percentage of budget authority	9.9%	20.4%	30.5%

Source: GAO review of agency financial reports and GAO calculation.

The three fee-funded agencies took different approaches to managing their unobligated balances. At the end of the fiscal years 2009 through 2012, USPTO, the Mint, and the FCC each reported large unobligated balances related to fee collections (see table 2). The origin of each agency's unobligated balance, and how each agency manages its unobligated balance, is related in part to how the fees were designed by Congress and the agencies.

U.S. Patent and Trademark Office's Unobligated Balances are a Long-term Strategy to Manage Revenue Instability

USPTO's $238 million unobligated balance at the end of fiscal year 2012 represents the agency's operating reserve. USPTO officials said that during the economic recession in fiscal year 2009, the agency experienced serious operational challenges as a result of a decline in the number of applications and patent renewals – and corresponding fee collections.[32] When collections are less than costs, USPTO faces a situation which impairs its ability to maintain operations, hire sufficient examiners, and invest in technology to handle a large backlog (approximately 591,000 patent applications as of July 2013). In 2010, to smooth the impact of economic downturns on operations and to help address funding uncertainty, USPTO announced its intention to designate a portion of Congress's annual appropriations as an operating reserve that could be carried over for use in future years. This reserve appears in USPTO's financial statements and OMB's budget database as an unobligated balance. USPTO officials said they do not intend to obligate these funds unless needed, and therefore USPTO will likely report

---

[32]Congress passed legislation in late 2010 that included a number of supplemental appropriations and rescissions affecting various government agencies. Included among them was a $120 million supplemental appropriation for USPTO. As a result of this supplemental appropriation, USPTO had access to almost all fees collected during fiscal year 2010.

unobligated balances every year. This operating reserve is separate and distinct from the Patent and Trademark Fee Reserve Fund established by the AIA, which is only available to USPTO to the extent appropriated by Congress and currently has no balance.[33]

In its patent fee rulemaking process, USPTO established and communicated a strategy to its stakeholders for developing the agency's patent operating reserve. In its proposed and final rules, USPTO included information on the intended size and funding strategy for the reserve. While developing this strategy, USPTO also sought and incorporated stakeholder input. For example, in response to comments from the public and from the Patent Public Advisory Committee, USPTO decided to slow the reserve's growth and to reduce the amount of fees designated for the reserve beginning in fiscal year 2013. In fiscal year 2013, USPTO issued a final rule reflective of this input and increased its patent fees, in part to fund a 3 month operating reserve (approximately $700 million) by fiscal year 2018. Specifically, the final rule adopted fees set at a lower amount compared to the proposed rule.

To determine the size of its reserve, USPTO used a risk assessment process to inform its decisionmaking, analyzing its operations and drawing on the reserve guidance from other organizations.[34] The two main factors that contribute to instability in patent operations are increases in costs and decreases in fee collections. Costs of patent operations consist mostly of the expense of patent examinations, and also include expenditures for information technology and general support costs. Collections consist of fees paid by patent applicants at different stages of the examination process and throughout the life of the patent: they vary with the speed of the application process (which is a function of

---

[33]The AIA created a second account, the Patent and Trademark Fee Reserve Fund. USPTO collections in excess of appropriations are to be deposited into this account. In the fiscal year 2012 appropriations, Congress provided USPTO with access to the funds in the Patent and Fee Trademark Reserve Fund; this was extended through FY 2013 by the continuing resolution. However, according to USPTO officials, there is currently no balance in the Reserve Fund.

[34] We recommended in April 2012 that USPTO finalize an operating reserve policy, including the expected level of reserves, to smooth the impact of economic downturns on operations and to ensure its use aligns with agency goals. The Department of Commerce accepted this recommendation. See GAO, *Patent and Trademark Office: New User Fee Design Presents Opportunities to Build on Transparency and Communication Success,* GAO-12-514R (Washington, D.C.: Apr. 12, 2012).

the number of examiners available), and with economic conditions both in the United States and in other countries. USPTO plans to assess the patent operating reserve balance against its target balance annually and, at least every 2 years, plans to evaluate whether the target balance is sufficient to meet USPTO's needs. According to agency officials, a similar reserve is planned for trademark fees, but the analysis to determine the appropriate size of the reserve is on-going; USPTO officials expect this analysis to be completed in fiscal year 2014.

The Mint's Unobligated Balance Represents a Reserve to Address Policy Changes, Collection Declines and Increased Costs

The Mint's unobligated balance is the source of the Mint's operating reserves, established in 2011 in response to operational challenges. Specifically, Mint officials said that they regularly review their open obligations, liabilities, projected earnings, and financial risks which include not having sufficient cash to meet required obligations, or sufficient resources needed to fulfill the mission appropriately. The Mint has had to take into account various factors, including (1) a decline in the Federal Reserve's demand for circulating coins due to the recession, (2) the Treasury Secretary's decision to suspend minting and issuing of $1 coins for circulation, (3) an increase in metal prices causing the Mint to lose money on the production of one-cent and 5-cent coins, (4) delays in release of numismatic products for sale, (5) decreasing demand for the Mint's numismatic products, and (6) increasing demand for the cash-intensive silver bullion coin program.

In response to these factors, Mint officials exercised their authority to suspend transfers of collections from the Mint's circulating coin revenues to the General Fund and, starting in fiscal year 2011, reserves were created from the unobligated balance as follows:

- Seignorage Reserve ($377.5 million as of August 2013): established to approximate one year's worth of circulating coinage operating expenses. This is to ensure continued delivery of coinage to the Federal Reserve Banks until other mitigating decisions or strategies are implemented to offset any effects that are impairing the continued financing of circulating operations
- Numismatic Reserve ($50 million as of August 2013): established to mitigate the risk of loss in revenue in sufficient amounts to cover cost should demand significantly decrease. The reserve represents the availability of funds for ongoing funding of approximately one year's funding of the Mint's protection activity. The protection activity is a cost without revenue to offset, and presents the most significant cost to fully cover should demand significantly decrease.

Mint officials said they will to continue to monitor Mint operations and the operating environment, including changes in customer demand, costs of inputs, administration policies, natural or man-made disasters, and critical investment needs, to determine if the reserves are at suitable levels for their purposes. These target levels were set at a level meant to reflect the needs and/or the risks that require mitigation over the next 2-5 years.

Federal Communications Commission's Unobligated Balance Largely Reflects the Timing of Collections and Outlays

Both FCC's salaries and expenses account, which contains regulatory fee collections, and USAC's USF contribution account had unobligated balances at the end of fiscal year 2012, with the USF account,[35] which includes Telecommunications Relay Service funds, containing much larger unobligated balances (approximately $3 billion) than the salaries and expenses account ($18 million). According to FCC officials, $10.4 million in unobligated funds in the salaries and expenses account is no-year funding and will be reapportioned in fiscal year 2013. Of the remaining $7.6 million, FCC officials said that $7.1 million will remain unobligated until FCC receives OMB and Congressional approval for special projects, and $500,000 relates to expired reimbursable authority. According to FCC officials, the salaries and expenses account's unobligated balances were regulatory fees associated with expired contracts or Recovery Act funds deobligated because contracts had not been signed.

Since fiscal year 2008, the FCC has not been provided access to its regulatory fee collections in excess of its annual appropriation. FCC's annual appropriation permits the agency to assess and collect regulatory fees up to a specified amount. This amount remains available until expended.[36] With respect to USF contributions, FCC officials reported that the approximately $3 billion in unobligated balances from USAC's

---

[35]USF collections are administered by the USAC, which is a non-governmental, private entity. As such, USF contributions are not subject to the appropriations process, unlike FCC's regulatory fee collections held in the agency's salaries and expenses account.

[36] In August 2012, we recommended that Congress should consider whether FCC's excess regulatory fees (approximately $66 million through fiscal year 2011) should be appropriated for FCC's use, or, if not, what the disposition of these funds should be, and whether to change FCC's annual appropriations language to permit reconciliation of excess collections or to govern FCC's handling of any future excess collections. Congress has not as yet taken any action. See GAO, *Federal Communications Commission: Regulatory Process Needs to Be Updated*, GAO-12-686, (Washington, D.C.: Aug. 10, 2012), 36.

GAO-13-820 Federal User Fees

USF amounts[37] was largely the result of the timing of collections and obligations for the four programs funded by USF contributions: (1) the Connect America Fund (also known as the High Cost program) for rural areas, (2) the Lifeline program (for low-income consumers), (3) the Schools and Libraries (or E-rate) program, and (4) the Rural Health Care program.[38] A significant length of time can lapse between contribution collections and the funding commitment. In the E-rate and Rural Health Care programs, the USAC does not record USF amounts as committed until the application is approved.

In addition to these timing issues, FCC officials said some USF contributions are set aside for specific multi-year pilot projects and appeals. Table 3 below shows the contributions, disbursements, and amounts set-aside in each program for fiscal 2012.

Table 3: Collections, Disbursements, and Set-Asides for Universal Service Fund Programs, 2012

	Connect America	Schools and libraries	Rural health care	Lifeline
Contributions received (CY)	$4.5 billion	$2.4 billion	$110 million	$2.3 billion
Disbursements to providers (CY)	$4.1 billion	$2.3 billion	$173.5 million	$2.0 billion
Unobligated balance (FY)	$ 1 billion	$1.7 billion	$136 million	$205 million
Reserves/set-asides (FY)	$805 million (for Connect America Fund implementation)	$683 million (for appeals and invoice extension requests)		$25 million (for broadband pilot)

Source: FCC

---

[37]USF contributions are paid monthly by telecommunications carriers (including landline and wireless companies, interconnected Voice over Internet Protocol (VoIP) providers, and other providers of telecommunications) based on their projected revenues. The contributions are collected by the Universal Service Administrative Company (USAC) an independent, not-for-profit corporation created in 1997 to collect universal service contributions and administer universal support programs.

[38] GAO, *Telecommunications: FCC Has Reformed the High-Cost Program, but Oversight and Management Could Be Improved*, GAO-12-738 (Washington, D.C.: July 25, 2012.); *Telecommunications: FCC's Performance Management Weaknesses Could Jeopardize Proposed Reforms of the Rural Health Care Program*, GAO-11-27 (Washington, D.C.: Nov. 17, 2010); *Telecommunications: Improved Management Can Enhance FCC Decision Making for the Universal Service Fund Low-Income Program*, GAO-11-11 (Washington, D.C.: Oct. 28, 2010); *Telecommunications: FCC Should Assess the Design of the E-rate Program's Internal Control Structure*, GAO-10-908 (Washington, D.C.: Sept. 29, 2010).

Considering Key Questions About Costs and Collections Can Enable Congress and Agencies to Identify and Manage Revenue Instability

The more a program or agency depends on fees to fund its activities, the more vulnerable it is to revenue instability: that is, the extent to which fee collections cover the intended share of costs over time.[39] Largely or wholly fee-funded programs do not necessarily see a proportional decline in costs when they experience a drop in collections. Absent access to other funding sources these program are sensitive to revenue instability, making the following considerations especially important.[40]

Key aspects of fee design can help or hinder agencies in managing revenue instability, and minimize or exacerbate the effect on the agency's ability to provide goods or services. The following key questions center on understanding (1) the data and analysis needed to identify and manage revenue instability, (2) the factors likely to affect collections, (3) the factors likely to affect costs, and (4) how agencies can manage fee revenue instability. They will be most useful when considered in conjunction with key questions for designing and implementing user fees: that is, how fees are set, collected, used and reviewed.[41] Appendix II provides a summary of the key questions discussed below.

What Data and Analysis are Needed to Identify and Manage Revenue Instability?

In order to identify and manage revenue instability, decision makers need regular information and analysis to understand potential vulnerabilities in the context of the specific fee design. The authority to create or implement a tool to manage revenue instability may be retained by Congress or it may be delegated to the agency. But regardless of where the authority lies, it is the agency's responsibility to obtain and analyze the necessary data to inform decision making. This is true even—or especially—in cases where statutory authority is required to act on the analysis.

---

[39] Ensuring that fees are set at a rate to cover the intended costs is referred to as revenue adequacy. We discuss the key considerations for ensuring revenue adequacy in GAO-08-386SP.

[40] Programs that rely solely on general fund appropriations can also experience fluctuations in funding, but the causes and considerations are distinct from those affecting fee-reliant programs.

[41] See GAO-08-386SP for the questions to consider when designing and implementing user fees.

Agencies should consider the following questions when gathering information for decision makers.

What is the risk that fee revenue instability will affect this program?

In considering approaches to managing fee revenue instability, an agency should develop a risk-based strategy. Risk assessment is the identification and analysis of relevant risks associated with achieving the program's objectives, and with forming a basis for determining how risks should be managed. Risk identification methods may include qualitative and quantitative ranking activities, management conferences, forecasting and strategic planning, and findings from audits and other reviews.

Once risks have been identified, they should be analyzed for their possible effect. Risk analysis generally includes estimating the risk's significance, assessing the likelihood of its occurrence, and deciding how to manage the risk. GAO's *Standards for Internal Controls in the Federal Government* notes that the specific risk analysis methodology used can vary by agency because of differences in agencies' missions and the difficulty in qualitatively and quantitatively assigning risk levels.[42]

The strategy developed to manage revenue instability should match the level of risk identified. For example, preparing for risks that are highly unlikely but would have dire consequences can result in a reserve balance that is unnecessarily high and draws revenue away from other fee program needs. In 2013, we found that for the Agricultural Quarantine Inspection (AQI) program, the Animal and Plant Health Inspection Service (APHIS) had based its target reserve balance on largely unrealistic risks—including the possibility of ceasing all inspections—and as a result, developed a target reserve balance that was unnecessarily high.[43] We recommended a reserve target that is more closely aligned with program needs and risks. United States Department of Agriculture agreed with the recommendation, and adjusted its target reserve balance to a level it said would allow for continuous services in the event of an unforeseen

---

[42] GAO, *Internal Controls: Standards for Internal Controls in the Federal Government,* GAO/AIMD-00-21.3.1. (Washington, D.C.: November, 1999.)

[43] GAO-13-268.

decrease in user fee collections, or other instances that could cause an increase in workload for the program.

What analysis should be performed and what data are needed?

The appropriate analysis can help an agency obtain a thorough understanding of factors such as cost drivers and elements that influence collections. As recognized in the *Statement of Federal Financial Accounting Standards 4: Managerial Cost Accounting Standards and Concepts*, agency cost information should be sufficient to be used by Congress and federal executives in making program and resources decisions, as well as for setting fees, but the analysis does not necessarily need to be complex, costly, or require special resources. Agencies should seek to leverage data and analysis that already exists. For example, agencies may use proxies, or leading or lagging indicators to forecast key changes, rather than undertake complex, original analysis to do the same. USCIS is almost entirely funded from immigration and naturalization application fees and uses data from DHS's Office of Immigration Statistics, among other sources, to project the volume of incoming applications.[44]

Are there limitations to the available data (such as preliminary estimates) that could add uncertainty to collection estimates?

Indicators that are drawn from early estimates may add vulnerabilities to demand or collection forecasts. For example, each quarter, Universal Service Administrative Company projects the next quarter's anticipated USF demand and assessable industry revenues. The FCC uses this information to determine the applicable contribution factor (percentage of assessable revenues) for the following quarter. FCC officials have found that their use of projected data in setting the USF contribution factor has led to collections that are more or less than initially expected.

How frequently should this analysis be conducted?

Once the necessary analysis has been identified, agencies should consider how frequently to perform the analysis. Although agencies are required to conduct biennial fee reviews per the CFO Act, revenue

---

[44] GAO-09-180.

instability may occur over a shorter time horizon and may demand more frequent examinations. In particular, agencies should balance informational and reporting needs with the cost of performing the analysis. For example, FCC reviews USF outlays, receipts, and cash balances monthly, and these are taken into account in the quarterly adjustment of the USF contribution factor.

What Factors Could Affect the Timing and Pattern of Collections?

Fee-funded agencies sometimes experience revenue instability as a result of how, or how frequently, fees are collected and external factors that can influence the demand for the goods or services. Agencies can plan for contingencies by understanding the factors affecting payers and external events affecting the collection process. Asking the following questions could help decision makers plan for contingencies.

How frequently are fees collected?

User fees are not always received at regular or predictable intervals throughout the year. The frequency of collections is sometimes related to how and by whom fees are collected and paid to the Treasury. For example, airlines collect international air passenger inspection fees at the time a ticket is sold, but remit fees to the government quarterly on behalf of the passengers. Collections that come in small increments on a rolling basis or late in the fiscal year may inhibit an agency's ability to identify patterns and fluctuations in collections in the aggregate, or may create cash flow challenges. For example, USCIS receives application fees throughout the fiscal year but enters into year-long contracts at the start of the fiscal year. Because of the kind of legal authority USCIS has to obligate funds, USCIS must have collections equal to the full contract value available for obligation at the start of the year. (See also: What is the timing and pattern of spending?)

What remittance compliance issues may exist, and what are the tools for ensuring compliance?

Agencies may not collect amounts they are owed because of external factors affecting payers or because of vulnerabilities in the remittance process. For example, the FCC adjusts contribution rates and payments due from telecommunication service providers quarterly; however, abrupt changes in a company's finances (such as bankruptcy) can affect the actual remittance amounts. On the other hand, CBP has lost an unknown amount of revenue because it does not verify that it collects applicable user fees for every commercial truck, private aircraft, and private vessel for which the fees are due.[45]

In the event payers do not remit fees in a timely manner, the agency may need tools such as penalties to ensure remittance compliance. For example, CBP can levy interest charges or deny landing rights to airlines for non- or late remittance of the international air passenger inspection fees.[46] Similarly, the FCC can place a delinquent payer of regulatory user fees or USF contributions in "Red Light" status, which results in withholding Commission action in any licensing or similar proceeding until the payment or other satisfactory arrangements are made.

What external known or unknown events could affect fee collections?

Understanding external influences – for example, weather, world events, or changes in technology— allows for the proper planning of resources or the use of limited funding in the face of changing revenue. For example, according to USPTO officials, economic activity, like a recession, is an important consideration when developing workload forecasts, primarily patent and trademark application filings. In addition to economic factors, officials stated that USPTO considers overseas activity, policies and legislation, process efficiencies, and anticipated applicant behavior when preparing estimates. Estimates of incoming workload are developed after researching and modeling these elements, which helps USPTO plan. There may be indirect influences as well. For example, a fee on imports may be tied to the exchange rate. When currency exchange rates are favorable, the demand for cheaper items from foreign countries may increase. In this example the fee revenue would go up, or conversely, it would go down with a weaker exchange rate. Programs should regularly conduct environmental scans to identify new influences, or significant changes to existing influences.

---

[45] GAO-13-268. In 2013, we recommended that the Secretary of Homeland Security establish internal controls to alert personnel when fees are not paid, and to use available information to verify that arriving trucks, private aircraft, and private vessels pay applicable inspection user fees.

[46] Penalties need to be strong enough to deter unwanted behavior but not so severe that they cannot practically be imposed. For more information on design of non-remittance penalties, see GAO-07-1131.

Program management decisions can also influence the level of demand for a fee-funded activity, for example, when services are delivered through a third party. In 2010, we found that FCC had allowed certain prepaid wireless providers to be eligible telecommunications carriers in order to expand the availability of its Lifeline program.[47] Both participation in the program and payments to providers increased, but the program's internal controls were not addressing the risks of the telecommunication providers' inconsistent adherence to applicant eligibility requirements.[48]

In programs where fees for some activities subsidize the costs for other activities, payers' overuse of the subsidized activity may affect the agency's ability to cover costs. For example, according to USPTO officials, USPTO has intentionally designed fees to encourage innovation by reducing up-front fees for patent applicants and imposing higher maintenance fees later in the process, after users have already obtained a patent. Moreover, higher than aggregate costs must be charged of applicants and owners that do not qualify for reduced fees as a small or micro entity applicant. However, if applicants pay only the lower application filing fee and then decide against maintaining the patent, the higher maintenance fees are lost to USPTO. Because USPTO incurs the same cost to process an application whether the patent is maintained or not, and because costs are fully recovered in the aggregate over time and not at each step in the patent process, USPTO's patent examination costs do not match collections if maintenance fees are not collected.

How quickly is a change in collection amounts likely to occur?

External events or changes to internal policies can affect collections, in either the short or long term. For example, USPTO officials said rates of

---

[47]GAO, *Telecommunications: Improved Management Can Enhance FCC Decision Making for the Universal Service Fund Low-Income Program*, GAO-11-11 (Washington, D.C.: Oct. 28, 2010).

[48]Since the release of our 2010 report, the FCC made efforts to address the risks of telecommunication providers' inconsistent adherence to applicant eligibility requirements. For example, the Lifeline Reform Order established uniform eligibility criteria for the federal Lifeline program, and required service providers to determine whether a subscriber was in fact eligible for Lifeline service, based on documentation provided by the subscriber, rather than allowing subscribers to self-certify their eligibility. See Lifeline and Link Up Reform and Modernization et al., WC Docket Nos. 11-42 et al., Report and Order and Further Notice of Proposed Rulemaking, 27 FCC Rcd 6656 (2012) (Lifeline Reform Order).

collections can change rapidly in response to economic events. During the 2009 recession, fewer patent applications were filed and maintained than were anticipated in the 2009 fiscal year, which reduced fee collections. Policy changes can affect collections as well, as when USCIS experienced a 100 percent increase in immigration and naturalization applications before USCIS increased its fees by an average of 86 percent in July 2007. Revenues can also be affected by market supply and demand. Further analysis can reveal whether fee changes are prudent based on the price elasticity of the good or service being provided, including whether there may be substitutes in the private sector.[49]

What Factors Can Affect Costs in Fee-funded Programs?

Fee-funded agencies should ask the following questions to gather information about the factors that affect their costs.

What are the fixed and variable costs of fee-funded activities?

If a fee is designed to recover all or a portion of the costs associated with an agency program or service, it is critical that agencies record, accumulate, and analyze timely and reliable data relating to those costs, consistent with applicable federal cost accounting standards. For example, according to USPTO officials, when USPTO began redesigning its fees under AIA in 2011, it used an activity-based cost accounting system to understand all agency costs as they relate to the activities performed supporting the fees collected. USPTO's Activity Based Information helps officials identify and analyze current activity costs on an ongoing basis, which helps with planning decisions as well as justifying budget requests.

What is the timing and pattern of spending?

Program management needs to understand the timing of program obligations in relation to the timing of collections during the fiscal year. As with collections, some agencies may have predictable patterns of obligations — whether regularly scheduled payments (such as payroll) or established spikes at particular points in the year (such as payouts for performance awards or bonuses). Other obligations may occur in a less predictable pattern.

---

[49] See GAO-08-386SP for more information about price elasticity and fee-funded programs.

Large upfront costs (such as IT investments or capital asset purchases) should be identified in time to capture those costs when setting fee rates, especially if the costs are ongoing (see also: *Develop and Maintain a Reserve Fund*). Fee-funded programs may require specific efforts to ensure that necessary infrastructure improvements are not neglected in cost accounting methods. For example, in 2007, USCIS stated in its fee review its intention to use all premium-processing fee collections toward investments in information technology and business-system transformation,[50] two planned infrastructure improvements.[51]

Can the agency quickly respond to changing costs?

Fee-funded programs may have flexibility to adjust program activities in response to rising costs, but certain types of costs create vulnerabilities if not considered in advance. For example, if fee-funded activities are inherently governmental in nature, and therefore required to be performed by federal employees, a reduction in fee revenue may be more challenging, because it takes longer to increase or decrease the number of federal employees than it would to adjust the number of contractors.

Data analysis can help program managers understand how quickly changes in costs could affect program activities. For example, USF sometimes experiences short-term changes in demand, stemming from program changes (such as the creation of pilot programs), revised eligibility rules, or program growth due to outreach efforts. The FCC and USAC regularly monitor potential changes in the level of USF commitments, and calculate the telecommunication companies' contribution levels on a quarterly basis. This allows USF collections to be more responsive to mid-year changes in obligations.

---

[50]Funding USCIS' information technology investments with premium-processing fees was consistent with Congressional report language accompanying the fiscal years 2008-2010 Department of Homeland Security appropriations bills.

[51]In December 2000, Congress authorized the collection of a premium processing fee in addition to the regular application fees for employment-based applications. Congress set the amount of the fee at $1,000 and directed that these amounts be available for (1) the premium processing activities and (2) infrastructure improvements associated with adjudications and customer-service.

What is the relationship between costs and revenue?

Without data analysis, it is difficult to fully understand the relationship between costs and revenue. If costs increase and there is no corresponding increase in collections, programs will likely experience a cost-collections gap that needs to be addressed. However, increasing costs are sometimes due to improvements in service delivery (which can be more expensive), and over the course of time may lead to increased revenue. For example, a USPTO official said that spending more on overtime can increase production, which in this case is increasing the number of patent applications being examined. Since fees are required for many responses during examination, the increase in overtime costs generates more fee revenue as a result of the increase in applications examined and the replies necessary.

Decision Makers Can Manage Revenue Instability By More Closely Aligning Fees and Costs and Using Reserve Funds

To manage revenue instability actively and ensure continuity of goods or services, fee-funded agencies can better align fees with costs and create reserve funds. First, ensuring that program costs and fee rates remain aligned will minimize the chance of a cost-collections gap over the long-term. If revenue instability is a function of a fee's design, the most sustainable solutions will be found by realigning costs and collections. Not all fee revenue instability can be completely addressed in this way, however, and some agencies may need to take additional action. Maintaining a reserve can help address sudden or temporary fluctuations in collections and/or costs, and can minimize the effect of revenue instability on operations. Reserve funds can both help manage revenue instability, and where appropriate, serve as a mechanism for accumulating revenue for identified future capital investments.

Closer Alignment of Fee Costs and Collections

To determine whether closer cost-collection alignment could sufficiently and timely address revenue instability, agencies should consider the following questions.

How quickly can the program adjust fee rates in response to changes in collections or costs?

Adjusting fees through either statutory or rulemaking processes can be a lengthy process, so it is important to plan ahead. Regular fee reviews ensure that Congress, stakeholders, and agencies have complete information about changing costs and whether a fee needs to be changed.

Are fees set at a rate that enables the program to respond to spikes or surges?

Fee reviews can help agencies determine if they are prepared for spikes or surges in demand, which may occur more or less frequently, depending on the good or service. Over-staffing or excess capital creates waste and establishes a higher-than-needed unit cost for the service; however 100 percent efficiency provides for no flexibility to address surge capacity.

Does the program have other sources of funding that may mitigate initial revenue shortfalls, or is the program fully fee-reliant?

Fully fee-funded programs typically experience some lag time before initial collections are realized. To cover costs before collections are realized, the program may require another source of initial funding. Congress has sometimes provided this initial funding through an appropriation that may or may not be reimbursed over time. If an appropriation is to be reimbursed, reimbursement is generally done through incoming fee collections.

Develop and Maintain a Reserve Fund

When the risks of revenue instability are greater than the agency can manage by aligning costs and fees, having a reserve can enable the agency to continue providing goods and services despite fluctuations in collections, and to act quickly in response to changing conditions. Reserve funds can also be a tool for fee-funded programs in planning for capital investments. Agencies should consider the following questions in developing a reserve fund.

What legal authority does the program or agency have to develop and fund a reserve?

Before an agency commits to building a reserve, agencies must understand their statutory structures. Agencies with no-year funds—that is, collections that remain available for obligation until expended – allowing the agency to carry over balances indefinitely. This gives the agency the flexibility to build or maintain an internal reserve fund within their existing fee accounts. Also, agencies with multiyear collections, or collections available for obligation for a fixed period of time beyond one fiscal year, may also be able to maintain a reserve fund. Absent those authorities, agencies would require additional authority from Congress to develop and maintain a reserve. If not specified in statute, agencies should verify their legal authority to keep funds in reserve.

Further, individual authorizing statutes may require or restrict a fee reserve. For example, the Consolidated Omnibus Reconciliation Act of 1985 (COBRA) requires CBP to maintain a $30 million reserve in the existing COBRA fee account, and the United States Department of Agriculture's AQI program is authorized to develop and maintain a fee reserve in the existing fee account.

Does the agency need to notify Congress or seek permission, beyond its existing authority, to use its reserve fund?

Money in the reserve may only be accessible up to a set amount or within a specified time frame. Decision makers can also limit use of the reserve in other ways, such as

- money in the reserve may only be available for specified purposes or in response to a trigger, like a natural disaster;
- agencies may only have access to reserves in specific amounts, such as a percentage at a time in order to avoid total depletion of funds, or
- agencies may be required to report on their level of use and their plan for ending their use of the reserve.

Alternative budget account structures like a reimbursable account or revolving fund could help mitigate budgeting or timing challenges without compromising accountability for federal funds.[52] Program managers may also consider what mechanisms exist within the agency to track reserve balances.

What is the goal of the reserve?

Regardless of the authority under which a reserve is created, setting clear goals for the reserve and clarifying how the reserve will be implemented helps ensure accountability and transparency both to Congress and users of fee-based programs. For example, some agencies may wish to use a reserve to help ensure the long-term financial stability of the agency or to position the agency to respond to varying economic conditions. Others may seek a reserve to smooth expected fluctuations in costs or collections, or to build capital for necessary infrastructure improvements.

---

[52] GAO, *Budget Issues: Better Fee Design Would Improve Federal Protective Service's and Federal Agencies' Planning and Budgeting for Security*, GAO-11-492 (Washington, DC: May 20, 2011).

Still other programs may seek a reserve as a means to mitigate unforeseen and unavoidable revenue shortfalls.

Historical data can demonstrate to Congress, to stakeholders, and to fee payers why a reserve is needed. For example, based on USPTO's experience with a rapid decline in collections during the recession in 2009, and to address other sources of revenue instability, officials told us they are building an operating reserve to avoid a slowdown in operations should collections suddenly decline. According to officials, the agency used risk assessments of spending levels and revenue streams to explain to stakeholders why fees were being increased to build an operating reserve. (See also: *What is the risk that revenue instability will affect this program?*)

Who should review and approve the reserve policy?

In addition to notifying Congress as part of a transparent communication strategy, reserve policies could be published and reviewed by stakeholders via the *Federal Register* notice and comment process or alternatively, by existing fee advisory boards or committees. Internal agency policies may also require review by cognizant financial officers.

What level of reserves should be maintained?

To ensure accountability and adherence to the reserve's goals, establishing minimum and maximum reserve levels may be advisable. These numbers should be justified with program data and risk management considerations. When established reserve goals have been achieved, such as to fund planned capital investments, the level of reserve should be assessed for reasonableness.

How should the reserve fund be built and at what pace?

Data analysis and communication with users should inform the rate at which funds are applied to the reserve, and what actions are taken when the desired level is reached. For example, USPTO estimated in January 2013 that the patent operating reserve would reach its target of 3 months of operating expenses in fiscal year 2018, after accumulating a proportion of patent fees over 5 years. As the operating reserve approaches its target, USPTO plans to consider the level of reserve in its biennial fee review. USPTO sought input from patent users and stakeholders in creating a reasonable timeline for building its reserve.

Concluding Observations

In 2012, the President's budget reported collections of nearly $300 billion in federal user fees, funding a wide variety of programs integral to our nation's security, to the security of our financial system, and to the protection of our natural resources. In light of the nation's current fiscal condition, it is essential that every funding source and spending decision be carefully considered and applied to its best and most efficient use. By their nature, federal user fees do not—and should not—follow a single model or design. However, wide variation can contribute to more challenging oversight. In light of this, it is critical for Congress and agencies to understand the implications of the key design decisions— each choice in isolation and also in the aggregate—to achieve a deliberate design that minimizes unintended consequences. Regardless of the fee design decisions made, Congress and agencies both have a role in effectively managing fee funded programs and ensuring that fees are designed to meet the goals of the program and are managed effectively.

The same prudent management standards should be applied to fee-funded programs as to those funded by general revenues. As such, unobligated balances in fee programs should be scrutinized. The federal budget's accounting structure can make it challenging to isolate unobligated balances resulting from fee collections, increasing the responsibility agencies have to manage and report on unobligated fee balances. Unobligated balances in fee programs may represent a reserve intended to manage the effects of revenue instability. However, to be effective as a reserve, agencies and Congress need to understand a fee's vulnerabilities and be deliberate in their design of a reserve fund to effectively manage them.

Agency Comments & Our Evaluation

We provided a draft of this report for review and comment to the Secretaries of Commerce and Treasury, and the Managing Director of the Federal Communications Commission (FCC). The Secretary of Commerce and the Managing Director of the FCC provided technical changes, which we incorporated where appropriate. We also provided a copy of the report to the Office of Management and Budget.

We are sending copies of this report to the Secretaries of Commerce, Treasury and the Managing Director of the FCC and interested Congressional committees. In addition, the report is available at no charge on the GAO website at http://www.gao.gov.

If you or your staff have any questions about this report please contact me at (202) 512-6806 or irvings@gao.gov. Contact points for our Offices of Congressional Relations and Public Affairs may be found on the last page of this report. GAO staff who made key contributions to this report are listed in appendix III.

Sincerely yours,

Susan J. Irving
Director for Federal Budget Analysis
Strategic Issues

Jacqueline M. Nowicki
Acting Director
Education, Workforce, and Income Security

Appendix I: Key Fee Design Decisions Allow for Agency Flexibility or Congressional Control

	Key design questions	Options increasing agency flexibility	Options increasing congressional control
Setting *For further discussion of setting user fees, see GAO's Federal User Fees: A Design Guide, p. 7.*[a]	**How are fee rates set?** *Congress specifies how specific fee amounts will be determined. This could include specific dollar amounts, rates or other requirements (such as provisions for exemptions, waivers, and caps).*	**By regulation** *Congress may grant the agency the authority to set fee rates by following the rule-making process spelled out in the Administrative Procedure Act.*	**In statute** *Congress may set fee amounts or rates in statute.*
Using *For further discussion of using user fees, see GAO's Federal User Fees: A Design Guide, p. 26.*[a]	**What Congressional action triggers the use of fee collections?** *Collections are classified into 3 major categories: offsetting collections, offsetting receipts and governmental receipts.*	**Offsetting collection authority** *Offsetting collections are authorized by law to be credited to expenditure accounts from which they may be obligated without further legislation. However, an annual appropriation act may limit the total amount an agency may collect during a given fiscal year.*	**Offsetting receipt authority** **Government receipt authority** *Offsetting receipts and government receipts are required by law to be deposited into receipt accounts. Whether government receipts can be used without additional appropriation depends on the specific authorizing legislation for the collection. Offsetting receipt collections may not be used without additional appropriations.*
	What is the period of availability for the collections? *Congress specifies the length of time for which collections are available for new obligations.*	**No-year** *No-year collections remain available for obligation for an indefinite period of time. A no-year appropriation of fee collections is usually identified by language such as "to remain available until expended."*	**Limited year** *One-year (fiscal year) or multiyear authority is available for a fixed period of time.*
	For what purposes may the collections be used? *Congress assigns the purpose(s) for which the collections can be used.*	**Broadly defined uses** *Congress may define the uses for particular collections broadly, for example, authorizing fees to be used for "all authorized activities and operations."*	**Narrowly defined uses** *Congress may define the uses for particular collections narrowly, authorizing fees to be used for specific, limited activities.*
	To what degree will Congress limit the amount of collections that can be used? *Congress sets the level of fee collections that the agency can spend in a given fiscal year.*	**No limit** *Congress may grant the agency the authority to spend all the money it collects without regard to amount or time.*	**Limit set in statute** *Congress may limit the amount of fee collections that the agency can spend to a particular dollar amount, often in annual appropriations acts. In some cases, Congress sets the limit and provides specific direction for the treatment of collections in excess of that limit.*

	Key design questions	Options increasing agency flexibility	Options increasing congressional control
Reviewing *For further discussion of reviewing user fees, see GAO's Federal User Fees: A Design Guide, p. 33.*[a]	**What types of reporting and oversight requirements are in place?** *Congress determines what type of requirements the agency must meet in order to permit the desired level of oversight.*	**Basic requirements such as CFO Act Biennial Fee Reviews** *Congress has designated basic review and reporting requirements. According to the CFO Act, the agency must review its fees on a biennial basis. This basic requirement applies for all 24 CFO Act agencies unless other requirements are specified for a particular fee program.*	**Additional requirements** *Congress may designate a number of additional requirements, such as reporting requirements and consulting with an advisory council. These requirements may be laid out in appropriations or authorizing legislation.*

Source: GAO.

[a]GAO-08-386SP.

Appendix II: Key Questions about Costs and Collections to Enable Congress and Agencies to Identify and Manage Revenue Instability

What Data and Analysis Are Needed to Identify and Manage Revenue Instability?

- What is the risk that fee revenue instability will affect this program?
- What analysis should be performed and what data are needed?
- Are there limitations to the available data (such as preliminary estimates) that could add uncertainty to the collection estimates?
- How frequently should this analysis be conducted?

What Factors Could Affect the Timing and Pattern of Collections?

- How frequently are fees collected?
- What remittance compliance issues may exist, and what are the tools for ensuring compliance?
- What external known or unknown events could affect fee collections?
- How quickly is a change in collection amounts likely to occur?

What Factors Can Affect Costs in Fee-funded Programs?

- What are the fixed and variable costs of fee-funded activities?
- What is the timing and pattern of spending?
- Can the agency quickly respond to changing costs?
- What is the relationship between costs and revenue?

Closer Alignment of Fee Costs and Collections

- How quickly can the program adjust fee rates in response to changes in collections or costs?
- Are fees set at a rate that enables the program to respond to spikes or surges?
- Does the program have other sources of funding that may mitigate initial revenue shortfalls, or is the program fully fee-reliant?

Develop and Maintain a Reserve Fund

- What legal authority does the program or agency have to develop and fund a reserve?
- Does the agency need to notify Congress or seek permission, beyond its existing authority, to use its reserve fund?
- What is the goal of the reserve?
- Who should review and approve the reserve policy?
- What level of reserves should be maintained?
- How should the reserve fund be built and at what pace?

Appendix III: GAO Contact and Staff Acknowledgments

GAO Contacts	Susan J. Irving, (202) 512-6806 or irvings@gao.gov Jacqueline M. Nowicki, (617) 788-0580 or nowickij@gao.gov
Staff Acknowledgments	In addition to the contacts named above, Chelsa Gurkin, Assistant Director, Steven Berke, Amber Edwards, Elizabeth Gregory-Hosler, Hayley Landes, and Felicia Lopez made key contributions to this report. Also contributing to this report were Virginia Chanley, Robert Gebhart, and Donna Miller.

Related GAO Products

Agricultural Quarantine Inspection Fees: Major Changes Needed to Align Fee Revenues with Program Costs. GAO-13-268. Washington, D.C.: March 1, 2013.

Federal Communications Commission: Regulatory Fee Process Needs to Be Updated. GAO-12-686. Washington, D.C.: August 10, 2012.

Patent and Trademark Office: New User Fee Design Presents Opportunities to Build on Transparency and Communication Success. GAO-12-514R. Washington, DC: April 25, 2012.

2012 Annual Report: Opportunities to Reduce Duplication, Overlap and Fragmentation, Achieve Savings, and Enhance Revenue. GAO-12-342SP. Washington, DC: February 28, 2012.

User Fees: Additional Guidance and Documentation Could Further Strengthen IRS's Biennial Review of Fees. GAO-12-193. Washington, DC: November 22, 2011.

Budget Issues: Better Fee Design Would Improve Federal Protective Service's and Federal Agencies' Planning and Budgeting for Security. GAO-11-492. Washington, DC: May 20, 2011.

Federal User Fees: Fee Design Characteristics and Trade-Offs Illustrated by USCIS's Immigration and Naturalization Fees. GAO-10-560T. Washington, DC: March 23, 2010.

Budget Issues: Electronic Processing of Non-IRS Collections Has Increased but Better Understanding of Cost Structure Is Needed. GAO-10-11. Washington, DC: November 20, 2009.

Immigration Application Fees: Costing Methodology Improvements Would Provide More Reliable Basis for Setting Fees. GAO-09-70. Washington, DC: January 23, 2009.

Federal User Fees: Additional Analyses and Timely Reviews Could Improve Immigration and Naturalization User Fee Design and USCIS Operations. GAO-09-180. Washington, DC: January 23, 2009.

Federal User Fees: Improvements Could Be Made to Performance Standards and Penalties in USCIS's Service Center Contracts. GAO-08-1170R. Washington, D.C.: September 25, 2008.

Federal User Fees: A Design Guide. GAO-08-386SP. Washington, D.C.: May 29, 2008.

Federal User Fees: Substantive Reviews Needed to Align Port-Related Fees with the Programs They Support. GAO-08-321. Washington, DC: February 22, 2008.

Federal User Fees: Key Aspects of International Air Passenger Inspection Fees Should Be Addressed Regardless of Whether Fees Are Consolidated. GAO-07-1131. Washington, DC: September 24, 2007.

www.ingramcontent.com/pod-product-compliance
Lightning Source LLC
Chambersburg PA
CBHW080618290526
45790CB00007B/2823